Our Exciting Earth!

CANYONS

I0800338

By Tanner Billings

Gareth Stevens
PUBLISHING

Please visit our website, www.garethstevens.com.
For a free color catalog of all our high-quality books, call toll free 1-800-542-2595 or fax 1-877-542-2596.

Library of Congress Cataloging-in-Publication Data

Names: Billings, Tanner, author.
Title: Canyons / Tanner Billings.
Description: New York : Gareth Stevens Publishing, [2023] | Series: Our exciting earth! | Includes index.
Identifiers: LCCN 2021039104 | ISBN 9781538275603 (Set) | ISBN 9781538275610 (Library Binding) | ISBN 9781538275597 (Paperback) | ISBN 9781538275627 (eBook)
Subjects: LCSH: Canyons–Juvenile literature.
Classification: LCC GB562 .B5 2023 | DDC 551.44/2–dc23
LC record available at https://lccn.loc.gov/2021039104

Published in 2023 by
Gareth Stevens Publishing
29 East 21st Street
New York, NY 10010

Copyright © 2023 Gareth Stevens Publishing

Editor: Kate Mikoley
Designer: Tanya Dellaccio

Photo credits: Cover Johnny Adolphson/Shutterstock.com; p. 5 Alexey Oblov/Shutterstock.com; p. 7 corlaffra/Shutterstock.com; p. 9 Meiqianbao/Shutterstock.com; p. 11 Gestur Gislason/Shutterstock.com; p. 13 silky/Shutterstock.com; p. 15 Anton_Ivanov/Shutterstock.com; p. 17 Damsea/Shutterstock.com; p. 19 Yongyut Kumsri/Shutterstock.com; p. 21 canadastock/Shutterstock.com; p. 23 Natural inspiration too/Shutterstock.com.

All rights reserved. No part of this book may be reproduced in any form without permission in writing from the publisher, except by a reviewer.

Printed in the United States of America

CPSIA compliance information: Batch #CSGS23: For further information contact Gareth Stevens, New York, New York at 1-800-542-2595.

Find us on

Contents

Big Canyons 4

Making a Canyon 12

Underwater Canyons . . . 16

Visit a Canyon! 18

Words to Know 24

Index. 24

A canyon is a big dip in land.

Some are huge!

They are deep.
The deepest is in China.

9

Canyon sides are steep.
They go right up.

Water cuts through rock.
This makes canyons.

It takes many years.

Some canyons are
in water.

You can see a canyon.
Many are in parks.

The Grand Canyon is one.
It is very big.

Let's go see a canyon!

Words to Know

rock

water

Index

China 8

parks 18

rock 12

water 12, 16

My State
SOUTH CAROLINA

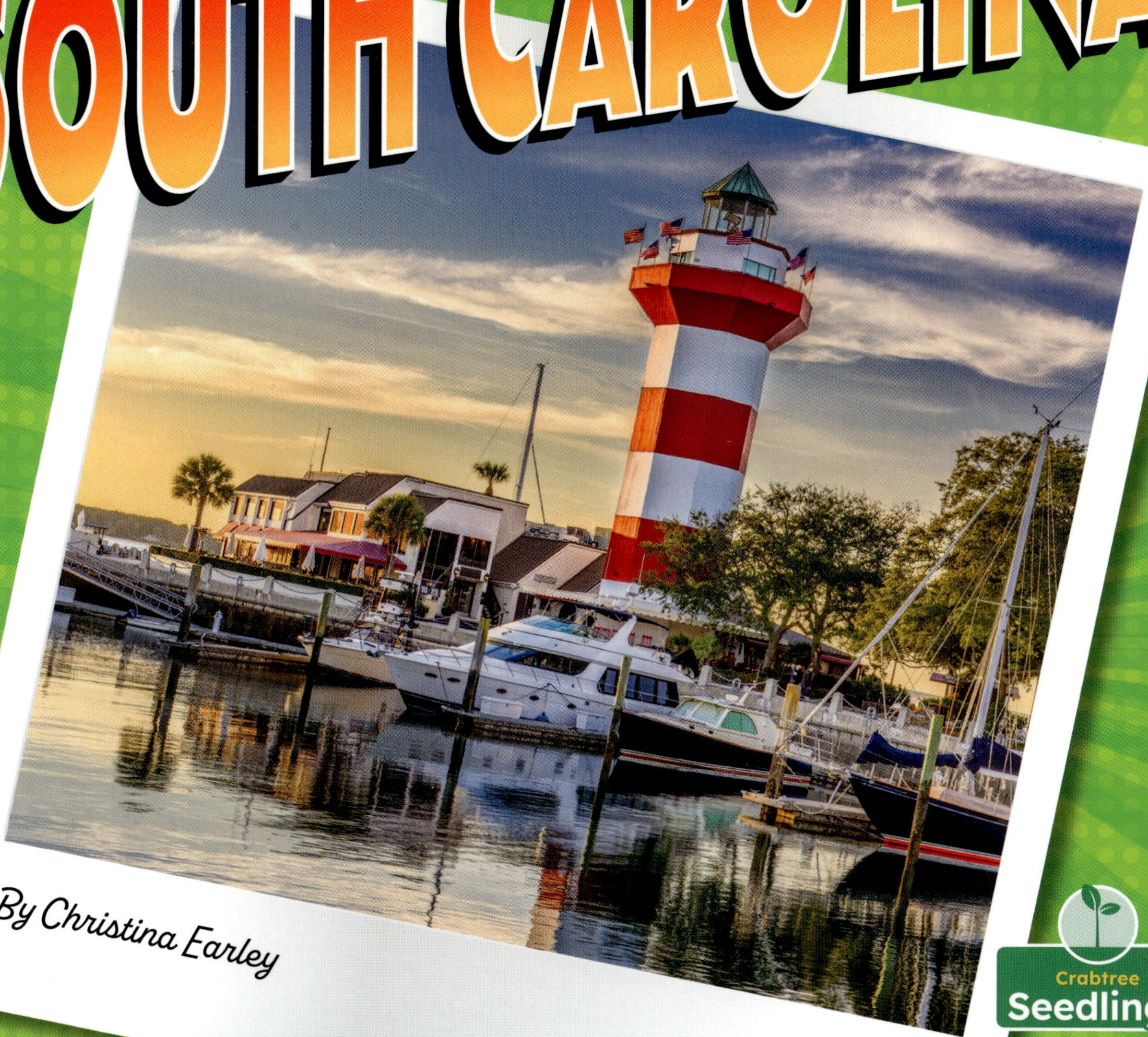

By Christina Earley

Crabtree Seedlings